Missing!

Stranger Abduction

Smart Strategies to Keep Your Child Safe

by Robert Stuber

Dignity®
Memorial

To locate a Dignity Memorial®
funeral service provider
visit www.DignityMemorial.com

ISBN: 0-8362-2635-6

Library of Congress Cataloging-in-Publication Data:
95-75866

*To my wife, Marsha, and
our two children.*

Contents

Chapter 2

Chapter 3

Chapter 4

Chapter 5

Chapter 6

Chapter 7

Chapter 8

Foreword

Here's a book that offers a potential for hope in the face of every parent's worst nightmare. The author skillfully pierces through our shock and denial by explaining in straight-forward terms both the reality of abduction as well as detailing in a clear methodological fashion the urgent matter of escape.

In keeping with the author's intent, parents should judiciously edit and adapt the material according to their own perception of their children's maturity and sensitivities. It is difficult to imagine a parent who would not appreciate access to the information presented here. The author encourages us to confront a devastating reality head on, and in so doing offers us a chance for hope when we need it most.

-- Terrence Hoffman, M.A.
Marriage and Family Therapist
Enloe Hospital Stress and Health Center
Chico, California

Introduction

After the initial release of <u>Missing!</u> in January of 1994, I was deluged with requests for radio and television shows and newspaper interviews. <u>Missing!</u> quickly went into its second printing. Having now the experience of talking with millions of parents, teachers, law enforcement officials, and children on the subject of child abduction, one common thread continues to surface. The fear that has grown and festered in the silence that has too long surrounded this issue quickly fades and is replaced by constructive ideas and pro-active attitudes as the dialogue is opened.

A few years ago I was at a shopping mall with my wife. Hanging in the window of a store was a poster so bleached by the sun that the only word readable from any distance was the word "Missing" in big letters which were once bright red, but had now faded to faint pink. The picture of the child and the rest of the information were all but gone. One of the things that made this sight so tragic was that the child had been missing less than a year. In less than twelve months, what was once a beautiful, energetic, youthful, dream-filled child had turned into a faded dust-covered poster hanging in a window that people like you and me walk by on a daily basis without noticing. My first reaction was to thank God that that wasn't *my* child's picture. Then I just wanted to go on about my business. A natural reaction, but somehow it didn't seem appropriate. As I stood there staring at the poster, the faded print was becoming slightly more readable. Date of birth, date reported missing, what the child was last seen wearing -- this wasn't just a poster, this was a little boy crying out for help.

"Please don't turn away from me. I need help. I didn't do anything wrong. I was playing in my front yard when someone grabbed me and now I'm lost. I want to come home. I miss my mom and dad and all my friends and my teacher too. I like cartoons and whenever I'm frightened I cry. The picture you're looking at is my

school picture. My dad took me to get a hair cut the night before it was taken...."

To my great surprise, what had moments earlier been no more than a faded reminder marking a tragic event, had been transformed into a personality, a life with a history as well as a future, clearly proclaiming his refusal to fade into the silence of denial along with the print of the poster. *"Don't pass me by, I will not go away."*

Child abduction is commonly referred to as a parent's worst nightmare. Although this may be true, it is also true that a nightmare only has power while one is asleep. Child abduction is not a nightmare, it is a reality and must be dealt with as a fact of life. In this context, the great silence that has governed this issue must be broken. Silence is the sleep upon which the nightmare thrives.

Missing! was written to be a catalyst for dialogue on the subject of child abduction. Through that dialogue we can move the issue from the realm of nightmare to reality. As a nightmare it paralyzes us with fear and therefore exists almost unchallenged. As a reality it can be beat.

By breaking the silence, you will be joining a growing army of parents and volunteers all across this country who have lived through this tragedy and have since dedicated their lives to making this world a safer place for all children.

There are missing children foundations all around the country. In most cases, these foundations were erected out of the ruins of a child's disappearance. They are staffed by parents, family members and volunteers. These dedicated heroes know better than anyone how to skillfully turn the nightmare of fear into the reality of constructive action. Most of these foundations are under-staffed and under-funded. They operate day and night, 365 days a year, driven by the hope that many children who are currently missing will be found. They are unwilling to let the lost become the forgottten. The first tragedy is when a child becomes missing. The greatest tragedy is when we allow that child to be forgotten.

For some reason, in this country we have a fascination with statistics. The government, industry, medicine, sports, nearly everyone uses statistics to determine what issues in our society are important, or to what degree they deserve our attention.

When it comes to children abducted by strangers, I have found that, depending upon who you talk to, the statistics change. The most important information one can gleen from a set a statistics can often be what the stats don't say.

The most optimistic statistics I could find on children abducted by strangers in this country says that between 400 and 450 children are taken every year. On the surface, those statistics seem to reflect a relatively small number, and in turn suggest that this is a small problem affecting only a small segment of our society.

What the statistics don't say is that most of these children have not been recovered. Many of these children are abducted from places where they were presumed to be safe. Their parents were not remiss in keeping a close eye on them. This happens across all socio-economic lines. Of the small amount of abductors that are caught, most are repeat offenders who have been in and out of prison for similar crimes against children.

Most importantly, the statistics don't say that this number represents an average of more than one child per day. That's too many.

-- Robert Stuber

How to Use this Book

The first line of defense is dialogue. Missing! is intended to help open discussion.

Fear is the enemy not the teacher. Don't try to scare children into being aware. Instruct them.

Not all the information in this book is right for every child. You, as the parent, are the expert. You decide what information is right for your child. The stories that follow each chapter are designed to help illustrate the information contained in that chapter in a manner to which a child can relate.

If you, the expert, feel that any of the stories are not appropriate for your child, then don't read them to him or her. Instead make up some of your own.

Don't overload your child. The subject of child abduction should be taught in the home regularly in small non-threatening doses.

Although this book deals primarily with escape and survival, things a child can use after an abduction has occurred, do not neglect to teach your child about prevention. (Chapter Seven has some suggestions.)

Many times parents and teachers have expressed to me how uncomfortable they have felt in trying to instruct their children in this subject. Their greatest concern has been about frightening the child.

The information you give the child is not what scares them. It's the manner in which you give it that determines whether or not you instill fear or empowerment. One of the greatest loved children's stories is about abduction. The Disney classic "101 Dalmations" deals not only with abduction but also the matter of escape. I mention this only to illustrate the fact that scary subjects can be taught in non-threatening ways. When information about child abduction is given to a child in a well thought-out, loving manner, that information can then be channeled by the child and parent in the direction of empowerment.

However, if the only time the subject is talked about is when the child or parent is witness to the frightening images of an abduction and search unfolding on the news, then the outcome is sure to be one of fear.

To be empowering, you have to be proactive. When children hear a news story of another child being abducted, rarely is it ever followed with any information of resolve. After the headlines, children are overloaded with frightening warnings from parents and teachers and then the issue is abandoned as quickly as it sprang up. This type of reaction is exactly what turns missing or lost children into faded-out dust-covered posters and allows the nightmare to continue. The missing turn into the forgotten, as we sit in silence, hoping to God that this never happens to us. When the missing become the forgotten, then every child becomes a victim.

How can you teach your child about abduction without scaring them? Be creative. You should try to instill awareness, not fear. If a child is aware, a situation that could be potentially dangerous will most likely never reach that critical point.

Being aware does not rob children of their childhood, it enhances it. You can teach awareness by playing games with your child. One father of a four-year-old told me that after reading this book, he began to teach his son the first steps of being aware by playing checkers with him. He told his young son to pay close attention to every move he (the father) made on the checker board, so that he would be able to tell when he was going to try and jump his men. From there he started discussing awareness of surroundings and other people.

Another parent told me that she was able to teach her seven-year-old daughter about the techniques in this book dealing with the trunk of a car while they were washing the family car together.

Never tell a child they might be abducted. Instead, teach the child things they can do if they ever need help or if they're in trouble.

Children know that bad things happen to people. This is an instinct that all of us possess; it's vital to our survival. Be cautious about sheltering your child too much from the realities of life.

When something bad like an abduction happens and it's broadcast on the news, never tell your child that it could never happen to them, or that mommy and daddy would never let that happen to them.

Instead, turn the tragedy into an opportunity to instill empowerment. Walk your child through the fear they may be experiencing. Tell them what they could do in a situation like that. Help them to understand the need to be safe all the time.

Most importantly, let them know that mommy and daddy will always do everything in their power to protect them and if they were ever lost, that you would never stop looking for them.

Jason

Nine-year-old Jason was a bright, outgoing, brown-haired, brown-eyed picture of youth. He liked football and comic books. His dad called him Buddy. One of Jason's jobs at home was to take the garbage out to the curb on Wednesday evenings.

On Wednesday evening Jason took out the garbage and was never heard from again. His decapitated body was found two days later in an empty field three blocks from his house. The autopsy showed that Jason had been sexually abused before being killed.

Jason knew everything a nine-year-old boy was supposed to know except, like so many other children, he didn't know how to protect or defend himself against child molesters or kidnappers. Jason's parents thought that teaching him about such things would be too intense at his young age.

Had Jason known the truth about these sick people, like the one who killed him, his chances of survival would have been greatly increased.

We teach our children about crossing the street and what happens to them if they are hit by a car. We teach them not to touch a hot stove and what happens if they get burned. We teach them how to stay warm on cold days and we teach them the dangers of smoking. But when it comes to child molesters and kidnappers, we simply teach them "Don't ever get in a car with a stranger." We do not teach our children enough!

More times than not, an abducted child is overpowered and thrust into a car or a house against his or her will. The first ten minutes after an abduction are the most critical. Thereafter, the odds of ever finding the child (dead or alive) begin to drop off dramatically. This book is written to help the child overcome the grim odds and return home to his or her loved ones.

What is the first thing a child should do once the abduction has started? Most of the time the child is not known to be missing until the abductor is miles away. What can the child do to possibly end this nightmare while still within a block or two of the abduction point? We'll address these questions in this book.

Once a child is known to be missing, the police and the community launch a massive search effort. Even though the search is the right thing to do, it is not enough.

The battle for survival is between the child and the abductor. The abductor is in control, not the police, the FBI or mommy or daddy. Second in command is the child. Will your child know what he or she is up against and what can be done to help bring about his or her rescue or escape?

Are you willing to face the truth about child abductors with your children?

The evil that is stalking our children must be met head on. Child molesters and kidnappers are everywhere. They live in our neighborhoods, teach in our schools, sit in the pews next to us in church, drive fire trucks, and shop at the same stores we do. They are like animals of prey with an appetite for young, defenseless children.

Once an abductor begins to stalk your child, chances are he will succeed. He waits in the shadows much of the time disguised as a respectable member of the community. He watches and plots while you go on with life as usual -- unaware of him or his intentions until, when the moment is right, he lunges from the shadows and your child is never heard from again. Our ignorance is the abductor's best cover.

How Much Should Your Child Know?

Even the Bible teaches that one should know the strength and intent of one's opponent before entering into battle. Knowing the strength and intent of an adversary is important because it dictates the degree of aggressiveness and method we will use in our struggle to survive.

The child abductor is twisted and sadistic. He wants to possess the child, separating the child from his or her family and environment. Getting the child alone, he inflicts fear, sexual abuse, beatings, and even dismemberment and death. Quite possibly he passes the child around to others for their twisted desires. The child may be brainwashed, or even chained up in a basement or in a cage like an animal for years. It doesn't take much of this treatment to break the will and warp the fragile mind of the child. Even if rescued, the child's life can remain a living hell.

The methods and scenarios contained in this book are presented as suggestions for your consideration in dealing with the tragic reality of child abduction. As the parent or teacher you are the final authority in deciding what information contained in this book is appropriate for teaching your child. Keep what you agree with, throw out that which you consider inappropriate, and better yet, come up with ideas of your own.

Chapter 1

Vehicles

It's a pretty sure bet to assume that if your child is abducted, he or she at some point will be transported in a vehicle, most likely a car, van or pickup truck.

This chapter deals with how to escape from a vehicle, disable it, or draw attention to it in order to increase the abducted child's chances of rescue.

Locks

Teach your child how to read the words "lock," "unlock," "open," "close," "on," "off." These words are used in various vehicles to label power door locks.

The child should practice locking and unlocking as many different vehicle locks as you have access to. He or she should practice opening the door and getting in and

27

practice opening the door and getting in and out by him or herself.

Teach the child how to turn the ignition key to the "ACC" (accessories) position. Although most power door locks can be operated without the key in this position, most power windows can not.

Windows

Teach your child how to read the word "window" and show him or her how to operate power and manual windows. Show the child the location of as many different power window switches as possible.

Sunroofs

Teach your child how to operate a sunroof. Let the child practice climbing out of every window in the vehicle including the sunroof, just like they would practice climbing out of windows at home in case of a fire.

Small children may be afraid to jump from a stationary car window. Practice will help them overcome their fear.

Practice Guide

If the child is abducted and left alone in a vehicle with the key in the ignition, he or she should have practiced the following tips you have taught to help escape an abductor. Be sure the child practices doing this.

1. Unlock the door (if successful unlocking the door, proceed to #4).

2. Turn the key to ACC.

3. Open the window.

4. Turn the key to off and remove the key from the ignition switch. Take the key with you.

5. Open the door or climb out the window.

6. Throw keys in the bushes, garbage or anywhere they won't be easily found.

7. Run to people or a good hiding place (see Hiding Places, page 87).

Make a plan and practice it often, just like a fire drill. In an emergency situation the child will most likely act according to the plan if you've practiced it enough.

Trunk

An abductor may lock his or her victim in the vehicle's trunk. Show the child what to do should that happen to him or her.

Show the child how to disconnect any exposed wires with his or her hands (or feet, in case the hands are tied). Disconnected wires will most likely cause the tail lights and brake lights to fail which will increase the probability of the vehicle being pulled over by the police.

Another tactic is to have the child continually kick the section of the trunk where the tail and brake lights are located. The repeated kicking stands a good chance of causing the lights to fail.

Teach your child that if the abductor's vehicle is pulled over or stops for any reason, to yell "help" loudly. If the child's mouth is gagged, tell the child to kick the roof or the sides of the trunk with his or her feet, or bump it with the head and continue to do so until someone comes or the car starts moving again.

Familiarize your child with tools and other things that might be carried in a trunk and how he or she can use them as a weapon later.

Have the child remove an article of clothing or find a rag so that if the trunk is opened by the abductor to check on the victim, the child may be able to hang the cloth out the trunk while it's being shut. The hanging material attracts attention while the vehicle is moving.

Wires

Wires should be grabbed tightly and yanked with a quick and powerful pull.

Kicking

Kick at the section of the trunk that is the rear of the car below the trunk lid, on the right or left side. This is where most tail and brake lights are located.

How to Disable a Car

Disabling a kidnapper's car serves several purposes. It draws attention to the vehicle, it possibly causes service personnel to get involved, and it can put the abductor with the child on foot. In short, disabling the car changes the abductor's game plan and increases the odds in the child's favor.

1. Teach the child that if he or she is forced into someone's car and cannot get out, that as soon as the vehicle starts to move, before it has a chance to pick up much speed, jump into the driver's lap kicking, screaming, and dislodging the driver's hands from the steering wheel. The intent of this maneuver is to cause the vehicle to run into something like a garbage can, mailbox, or parked car, which would disable the abductor's vehicle or involve

other people. This maneuver should only be attempted at very low speed. It does involve the risk of injury to the child and others. You as the parent need to decide whether the benefit outweighs the risk.

Practice this maneuver in a stationary vehicle in the driveway starting with the child in the front seat, then the back seat. If this maneuver is carried out successfully, and with a little bit of luck, an abduction may well never get more than a block or two from its origin without anyone getting hurt.

2. If the child is left alone in the vehicle at any time, he or she can try the button maneuver to disable the vehicle.

Pull off the smallest button on his or her clothing. Insert the button into the ignition slot where the key goes. Push the button in as far as possible (use another small object to push the button in if needed and available). This should prevent the key from going in the ignition switch so the abductor will be unable to start the vehicle.

You may want to sew a couple of extra buttons inside the child's clothing just for this purpose. Check and make sure the button is the right size.

3. Show the child how to reach up under the dashboard on the driver's side and grab a handful of wires and pull them as

hard as he can to break them loose. This should render the vehicle immobile. This maneuver works on most vehicles and can be performed even while the vehicle is moving.

4. If the child is left alone in the vehicle and maneuvers two and three can't be performed and the child cannot escape, then teach the child how to flood the engine. Show the child where the accelerator pedal (gas pedal) is. Show him or her how to pump the pedal to cause the engine to flood. This is done by pumping the pedal repeatedly and quickly for as long a period as possible. This will not work on vehicles with fuel injection, which include most cars made since the mid-1970s.

Once the child begins this procedure, he or she should continue to check to see if the abductor is returning to the vehicle. If not, continue pumping the pedal until the abductor is seen. A flooded engine will not start right away. Many people who try to start a flooded engine inadvertently flood it more. This could cause the battery to run down, draw attention to the vehicle, and even cause service personnel to get involved.

5. Teach your child how to jump to the floor and push down the accelerator pedal when the abductor is stopped at a signal.

This should only be attempted if the abductor's vehicle is stopped close behind another vehicle. This could cause the vehicle the child is in to rear-end the one in front of it; drawing attention to the abductor's vehicle. The abductor's license plate number is likely to be taken and the police may be summoned. The abductor's vehicle may also be disabled.

Despite the obvious risk of injury to the child and others, the odds of surviving an accident of this nature are better than surviving in the abductor's hands.

Headlights

If at all possible, have the child turn on the headlights in the daytime. There is a chance this could cause the battery to run down and involve service personnel. Teach the child how to operate headlight switches in various vehicles.

Drawing Attention While in a Moving Vehicle

1. Write the word "help" backward on a foggy window. Teach your child how to write the word help in a mirror image.

2. Throw stuff out the window. If your child has access to a piece of paper or something, he or she can tear it into multiple

pieces and drop a piece out the window every few seconds. Also, if possible, hang the seat belt out the door. The litter and the hanging seat belt stand a good chance of attracting the attention of a police officer.

3. If the abductor allows the child outside the car such as for a roadside rest, the child should first, if possible, run to someone for help or scream for help if others are around to hear. If no one else is around, show the child how to use a rock, belt buckle, or any other object to scratch off the renewal date sticker on the rear license plate. This will add to the odds of being pulled over by the police.

4. Have the child pick his or her nose until it bleeds, then let the blood drip all over his or her clothing. People who see the blood-stained clothing will be alerted. The blood can also be used to write help on the arm or hand.

The abductor may decide to stop to discard or clean the blood-stained clothing, or go to a store and replace the clothing. This creates opportunities for escape or rescue.

Bobby

Bobby Wilson is a little boy six and a half years old. His hair is almost white and his parents keep it cut in a flattop. Bobby likes it short because he never has to comb it. Mrs. Wilson, Bobby's mother, works at a bank. His father is a grocery store clerk. Bobby has a dog named Digger. He named him Digger because the dog's always digging holes in the yard.

It was Saturday morning and Bobby was excited because his mother was taking him shopping and out for lunch.

Mrs. Wilson was putting on her makeup. "Would you bring in the mail?" she asked. "Sure," Bobby replied, and out the door he ran. The mailbox was on the street corner in front of the house. Bobby ran down the front porch steps out to the end of the driveway to the mailbox. He reached inside to get the mail.

Just then a big blue car with a male driver pulled up. The man held a piece of paper in his hand and said to Bobby, "Excuse me, but I think this letter belongs to you." Bobby stepped over to the car as the man inside opened up the door. "Do you want it?" asked the man. "Yes, please," Bobby answered. As Bobby reached for the paper the man grabbed Bobby's hand, pulled him into the car, and sped away.

Bobby was very scared and screamed "Let me out, let me out!" The man just laughed and drove while holding Bobby by the arm.

As the car slowed down to turn a corner, Bobby jumped into the man's lap and started hitting and scratching him. The man lost control of the car and ran into some garbage cans that were placed on the curb. All the neighbors came running out of their houses when they heard the noise.

The man pushed Bobby back into his seat and quickly drove off. He yelled at Bobby, "If you ever do that again I'll kill you." Bobby was so afraid he started crying.

The people on the street corner where the garbage cans were called the police. They told police what happened. They told them what the car looked like, which way it went, and said there was a man and a little white-haired boy inside. One person even remembered the license plate number.

Bobby and the abductor had been driving now for about four hours and Bobby was getting very hungry.

Bobby's parents had called the police once they realized something was wrong. The police, together with the neighbors, organized a search effort. The police told Mr. and Mrs. Wilson about the incident that happened with the garbage cans ealier that day over on the next block, and that the description of the boy in the car matched that of Bobby.

The police put out an all-points bulletin with the description of the car and Bobby, and the license number. Now police all over the state were on the lookout.

As the sun was starting to set, the abductor pulled into a gas station that was out in front of a shopping mall. By now they were about four hundred miles away from where Bobby lived.

The man told Bobby to stay in his seat while he got out to pump the gas. After the man got out of the car, Bobby carefully reached over with his foot and began to pump the gas pedal. Bobby's father had taught him that pumping the gas pedal too much would flood the carburetor and make it hard to start the car. Bobby watched the man while continuing to pump the gas pedal. When the man finished putting gas in the car, Bobby stopped and moved over to his seat.

When the man got in the car and tried to start it, it would not start. He started pumping the gas pedal faster and faster, not knowing that Bobby had flooded the engine.

As he continued to try starting the car, he became angrier and angrier. The battery was starting to run down. People at the gas station were looking at him. The station attendant came over to ask if he could help.

The kidnapper jumped out of the car in a fit of rage and opened the hood to see what the problem was. While the kidnapper was looking under the hood, Bobby opened the door, got out of the car and ran inside the gas station where the cashier was. Bobby told the cashier that he had been kidnapped. The cashier believed him. She took Bobby behind the counter, locked the front door, and called the police.

By the time the kidnapper realized that Bobby had escaped, the police were already pulling into the driveway of the gas station. The kidnapper was arrested and Bobby was returned safety to his parents.

Isaac

Isaac was abducted from a shopping mall during a brief moment while he was waiting for his mother to finish using the restroom. Isaac is six years old and he's been missing for two days.

He was abducted in California. The man who took Isaac is driving to Florida to trade him to some drug dealers for a debt he owes. The drug dealers plan on using Isaac for child pornography.

They travel at night. During the daytime, they stop in secluded country areas so the abductor can sleep. When he's sleeping, he puts a chain around Isaac's leg. The chain is about ten feet long. He locks the other end of the chain to the rear bumper of the car. Isaac can walk about five steps.

On the second morning as the abductor slept, Isaac was chained to the rear of the car. He sat in the dirt and tried to stay in the shadow of the car as the day began to heat up.

Isaac was frightened. He passed away the hours crying or trying to sleep. What frightened Isaac the most was his teacher had just been talking about child abductors and he knew from what she had been saying that they were going to hurt him; he might not ever see his mom and dad again.

Isaac didn't like thinking about these things, but he couldn't get them out of his mind. Every time he woke up from a nap, the scary thoughts would start racing through his mind again.

As he was sitting and doodling in the dirt he blankly stared at the rear of the car. Going over and over in his mind were things his teacher had been saying. Suddenly he remembered what she had said about ways of helping the police find you.

The license plate, that's right, what did she say about the license plate? Isaac thought excitedly to himself. Then he remembered "scratch off the number tag." That's what she said, "scratch off the number tag." Quickly Isaac began to look around for something to use to scratch off the number tag. He didn't know why he was supposed to do it, he just knew his teacher said it would help the police find him.

Isaac found a pointed rock and started to ever-so-slowly scratch at the tag until it was gone. There was another tag under that one but he didn't have time to do anything with that one because the abductor was waking up. Isaac threw the pieces of the tag under the car so the abductor wouldn't find them. The sun was starting to set and Isaac and the abductor were once again on the move.

They had been driving for several hours. It was dark and windy outside. They were on a freeway with lots of other cars. All at once Isaac noticed the red glow of police lights coming from the rear of the car. The abductor grabbed Isaac hard by the arm as he was slowing down to pull over. "You just sit there and keep your mouth shut or I'll cut your throat," he bellowed. Then he released Isaac's arm as they came to a stop.

At first Isaac didn't know what was going on, then he turned around and saw the police car behind him. He thought about the number tag he scratched off the license plate and knew that this was his chance to get away.

The police officer walked up to the car and asked the man for his driver's license and registration. As the man was searching in the glove compartment for the registration, Isaac quickly unlocked the door and jumped out of the car yelling, "Help me, help me! I've been kidnapped!" The officer pulled his gun out, pointed at the man and told him to freeze.

Later at the police station, the officer told the abductor that he pulled him over because he didn't have a correct registration tag on his license plate.

Isaac got to ride home on an airplane with a policeman back to his family.

Brandy

Eight-year-old Brandy was abducted on a Sunday morning as she was walking home from Sunday school. She was walking with her girlfriend. They got to her friend's house and said good-bye. Brandy continued to walk alone the half block to her house.

As Brandy was walking, a car pulled up along side of her. The woman driving the car got out and asked Brandy where the school was. As Brandy answered, the woman grabbed Brandy, forced her into the car, and drove away. When they came to a deserted road, the woman tied Brandy's hands and feet, put tape over her mouth, and put her in the trunk.

They traveled for a long time. Brandy was frightened and sore because every time the car hit a bump she would bounce around and get bruised. The car stopped twice for a short time. Each time it stopped, Brandy would kick the side and top of the trunk, hoping that someone would hear her and save her. No one ever came to her aid.

Brandy had been in the trunk for what seemed like forever. She was hungry, tired, and most of all scared. Her side was beginning to ache from lying in one place. She stretched her arms and legs out as far as she could to try and stop the ache, when her fingers touched some wires that were running along the side of the trunk.

Brandy knew what the wires were for because her father had taught her things to do if she were ever in this situation. Even though her hands were tied, she followed the wires with her fingers down to where they connected to the tail lights. With a quick hard pull, she broke the wires free from the tail lights. She maneuvered herself around and did the same thing on the other side of the trunk.

After a while Brandy felt the car come to a stop. She could also hear what sounded like another car engine running right outside the trunk. She started kicking the side of the trunk with her feet. She was trying to make as much noise as she could. Suddenly the trunk opened and there stood a policeman. He reached down and removed the tape from her mouth, then he untied her and helped her out of the trunk.

The policeman told Brandy's parents that he pulled the car over because it had no tail lights.

Chapter 2

Escaping from or Drawing Attention to a House

A house is probably the most difficult place to escape from. This chapter deals briefly with escape techniques and more extensively with ways to draw attention to the house. Drawing attention to or sending a message from the house is most likely to be your child's best strategy.

The abductor is likely to have the house well fortified against escape. However, it's important that the child has an idea of how to escape should there be an opportunity. The child should be aware of escape techniques to try when the abductor is gone or sleeping.

Closet Walls

Teach the child how to write "Help -- Kidnapped," and his or her name. This can be written on closet walls which reduces the chances of the abductor seeing it. The words can be scratched into the wall with a belt buckle, shoe buckle, coat hanger, etc. Teach the child to write this with big letters. This message may be found by the next people who use the room or house (assuming the abductor is on the move).

S.O.S.

During the abduction it is quite possible the child will be locked in a bedroom. Teach your child how to signal S.O.S. with the light switch.

S.O.S. is an international distress signal for help. It was originally broadcast by Morse code over the telegraph by three short dots (dit-dit-dit for S), three long dashes (dah-dah-dah for O), and three more short dots for S. This is done repeatedly (dit-dit-dit-dah-dah-dah-dit-dit-dit-dah-dah-dah-dit-dit-dit-dah-dah-dah-dit-dit-dit, etc.). S.O.S. is known to stand for save our souls, or on vessels, save our ship.

Teach your child to open the curtains at night and flash S.O.S. with the light switch five or more times and to do this every night. There is a good chance someone will see the signal and investigate or call the police.

Windows

Teach your child how to unlock and open as many different house windows and locks as you can. Let them practice climbing out the window.

Doors

Teach your child how to unlock all kinds of door locks including screens and sliding door security devices.

Toilet

Tie both socks or something else in a big knot and then place them snugly in the toilet bowl trap. Fill the bowl with paper and flush. This should cause the toilet to overflow and keep running.

The mess may alert neighbors downstairs, apartment managers, hotel guests, and may even involve a plumber. Also the overflowing toilet may preoccupy the abductor long enough for the child to escape.

Telephone

Dial 911 and tell the operator "I've been kidnapped!" That is all the child has to do. Do not hang the phone up! Set the receiver down. In most cases, the 911 operator can trace the call to the address and send the police.

Help (in a Mirror Image)

Teach the child how he or she can make their nose bleed. If nothing else is available, blood can be used to write "help" backwards in a window, or on a bed sheet or on a pillow case for a hotel maid to find. Bowel movement can also be used for writing.

Garbage

Teach the child to write "HELP -- POLICE."

This can be written on just about anything whenever possible and put in the garbage in hope the collector will see it and summon help.

Sharon

Sharon was seven years old when she was abducted walking home from school. She's been missing for nine months. Her parents, friends, neighbors, and the police have been searching for her everywhere. Her birthday was three months ago. Now she's eight years old and misses her family very much.

The man and woman who took Sharon keep her locked in a bedroom in their house in the same town Sharon lives in. There are no phones in the house and nobody ever visits. They make her eat in the bedroom and only let her out to use the bathroom.

One day after Sharon had been lying on the bed crying for a long time, she suddenly remembered something her mother told her to do if she ever needed help. Her mother had taught her how to send a help signal by turning the light off and on in a certain way. The signal is called an S.O.S. All this time she had been wishing she could get to a telephone to call the police and had forgotten about the S.O.S. signal.

Sharon decided that starting tonight, after the man and woman went to bed she would start using the bedroom light to send the signal.

The house was in a rundown area. Her barred bedroom window faced the backyard. Behind the house were some train tracks and an empty field. On the other side of the field was a lumberyard.

Night after night Sharon would wait for the man and woman to go to bed so she could open her window curtain and flash the room light to send the S.O.S. signal. First she plugged the space under her door with clothes so no one inside the house would see when she had the light on. Then she would flash three short flashes, three long flashes, and three short flashes repeatedly until she got too tired. Sharon did this for two weeks and was becoming discouraged because no one had rescued her.

Across the field at the lumberyard a night watchman had noticed the flashing light but thought it was a tree blowing back and forth in front of a street light or something like that.

One night when there was no wind and everything was still, the night watchman noticed the flashing light again. He realized there was no wind blowing trees in front of a street light. He was curious. The flashing pattern of light was familiar to him. He remembered the S.O.S. signal from his younger days when he was in the Navy.

The watchman called the police and showed them the flashing light. The police decided to investigate and went to the house. The police arrived at 3:00 a.m. They knocked on the door, calling out "police officer." The man inside awakened and opened the door. Sharon heard the police and screamed "help me, help me!" An officer rushed upstairs to her room.

The man and woman were arrested and taken to jail. Sharon was reunited with her family.

Juan

When Juan was abducted he was playing catch with his older brother and two friends in his backyard. One of the boys accidentally threw the ball over the fence into the alley behind the house. Juan climbed the fence to get the ball and he hasn't been seen since.

Juan is twelve years old. He's been missing now for three months. He's being kept somewhere in an upstairs apartment. He has to sleep locked in a closet. During the daytime he's allowed out of the closet but he has to stay in the same room with the abductor. Whenever the abductor leaves, he locks Juan back in the closet.

Sometimes the man makes Juan touch him in his private places. Sometimes he makes him walk around the apartment with no clothes on. Juan doesn't like doing this but whenever he complains about it, the man puts a gag in his mouth and beats him with a belt.

Juan desperately wants to escape but the man is watching him too closely. One day while he was out of the closet watching TV in the living room, he noticed a black marking pen on the coffee table. Very carefully he hid the pen in his shoe. That evening when he was back in the closet, he tried thinking of a way to write a note to let someone know where he was. He had no paper. How, he wondered, would he get the note out of the house anyway?

He remembered when his mother was washing his baby sister's diaper she accidentally flushed it down the toilet. The toilet overflowed and a plumber had to come and get the diaper out. Juan thought maybe he could flush something down the toilet to make it overflow. If a plumber came to fix it, maybe he would find a note Juan wrote.

Juan decided to write "help" and "closet" on his socks. Then he tied them into a ball. When the man let Juan out to use the bathroom, Juan stuffed the sockball into the toilet, filled the bowl with paper, and flushed it. The toilet overflowed just like he hoped. Water flowed from the bathroom floor onto the carpet in the hallway. When the abductor saw what was happening, he slapped Juan and put him back into the closet.

He tried to use a plunger but it was no use. He had to call the apartment house manager. Before calling the manager, he tied Juan up and stuffed a rag in his mouth so he couldn't make any noise.

After the manager removed the socks from the toilet he thought it was odd someone would tie the socks into a ball and flush them. He untied the socks and saw the words "help" and "closet." The abductor had been sitting in the living room while the manager was working on the toilet. When the manager got back to his own apartment he called the police. He knew something was wrong because of the message written on the sock and because the socks belonged to a child. He knew no child lived in that apartment.

Juan just celebrated his thirteenth birthday at home with his family and friends.

Chapter 3

Telephones

Private

The best way to send a signal to the police on a private phone is to call 911, say "help," and leave the receiver off the hook. By leaving the phone off the hook the police, in most areas of the country, are able to trace the call. Do not try talking to the operator unless the abductor is not around.

Don't hang up the phone. If a 911 call is made and the phone is then hung up, chances are the operator will call right back to see if everything is all right. This could alert the abductor and further jeopardize the child.

Leaving the phone off the hook increases the chances of a police officer being sent to investigate.

Be aware, some phones are not hooked to the 911 emergency service.

Try to leave a piece of clothing very close to the phone, preferably a shoe or sock because they are easily identified as a child's by anyone investigating the calls. The phone will be the focus of the 911 investigation.

The abductor will put the child out of sight from the 911 investigator who will be wanting to know who made the call. The abductor will most likely deny making it. The investigator will want to know whether anyone else is at home. Should the abductor claim no one else is home, then two possible scenarios can arise.

1. If the child has a chance to say "help" or anything else to the 911 operator, then the officer will have been told that a child had made the call. If the abductor says no one else is there then the officer will ask about the child heard on the phone by the dispatcher. At this point the officer should be suspicious enough to investigate further.

2. If the child was unable to speak to the 911 operator but was able to leave something easily identified as belonging to a child next to the phone which the officer sees, then combined with the abductor's claims that no one else is there, the officer should become suspicious.

Public Telephone

Using a public telephone can be tricky. Pay phones are hard to use and difficult for many children to reach. If the child has time to use a public phone, he or she probably has time to find a hiding place or go to someone for help. However, if using a public phone is the best choice for the child, he or she should try the following.

As always, dial 911. No coins are required to phone this number. When the operator answers say "help." Drop the receiver, slip off a shoe and leave it in the phone booth, then run and hide or summon help. Inside your child's shoe write with a laundry marker the child's name, phone number and "police." Even if the victim returns to the custody of the abductor, the information in the shoe can help the police track the kidnapper.

If the abductor is traveling, the other shoe can be left as a clue later; or use another article of clothing such as a belt or headband containing the same message. Sew easily detachable labels with this message inside their clothing so they can be used for the same purpose. The clothing and labels can be left anywhere, not just at public phones. Restaurants, service stations, and inside other cars are a few places the labels can be left. The message can even be handed to other people.

Leon

Leon asked his mother if he could go home with a new friend he met at school. His mother said he could but she would drop him off there because she wanted to meet his friend's parents first. They lived on the next block in a comfortable well-kept house.

Leon's mother met his new friend's parents and told Leon she would be back at four o'clock to pick him up. When she arrived at 4:00 to pick him up, they told her that Leon left for home at 3:30.

Leon hasn't been seen for three days. The man and woman of the house where Leon was playing had him locked in the backyard. They were part of a cult and used little children in their rituals which always resulted in the death of the abducted child. Their own children were too afraid to tell anybody what was really going on.

Leon was taken to a house in another part of the state where he was to be kept until the ritual. The people who were holding him treated him well. They let him watch TV and fed him good food. As Leon was sitting on the couch watching TV with the abductors, he noticed the phone on the end table next to the couch.

Leon's mother had taught him how to call 911 in case of an emergency. One time he called 911 just to see what would happen. When the dispatcher answered he got scared, dropped the receiver on the floor, and ran outside so that no one would know he was using the phone.

About ten minutes later a police officer showed up at his house and told his mother someone had called 911 from this phone number and asked if everything was all right. When Leon's mother and the police officer finally figured out what had happened, his mother scolded him and told him that 911 was only to be called in the event of an emergency. The police officer explained to him how the dispatcher can trace 911 calls to the address from which they are made even when the phone is left off the hook and no one is talking.

When the kidnappers left the room for a moment, Leon picked up the phone, dialed 911, and set the receiver down. He also took off his shoes and set them next to the phone.

His mother always wrote his name and phone number in his shoes. She told him that if he ever needed help and didn't remember his phone number, to look inside his shoe. Leon thought if the police came to check on his phone call and the kidnappers were hiding him, maybe the police would find his shoes by the phone and see his name inside.

About 15 minutes later someone knocked on the door. The kidnapper put his hand over Leon's mouth and carried him to the back bedroom. His woman friend opened the door and greeted police who were there to investigate the 911 call. The woman told the officer no one called.

The officer checked with the dispatcher on his radio to find out whether he had the right address. The dispatcher told him it was the right address and that the phone was still off the hook. The officer was invited to check the phone and saw Leon's shoes. He asked the woman if one of her children might have called 911. She said she didn't have any children. The officer knew something was wrong because the shoes belonged to a child. He looked through the house and found Leon and his captor in the bedroom.

Leon was taken home safely. All the people involved in his abduction are now in prison.

Chapter 4

How to Tell a Stranger What's Happening to You and Ask for Help

Most parents teach their children not to talk to strangers. However, during an abduction, the child must feel comfortable talking to strangers because it may require a stranger to save the child's life.

I believe we should teach our children not to talk to strangers, but the lesson has to be deeper than that. We have to teach them that there are good strangers as well as bad ones.

Children can become easily confused. Trying to choose a good stranger over a bad one can be quite difficult for a young child since children basically trust everyone.

In an emergency situation, such as an abduction, the rules change. Your child must know and feel comfortable with this change. During an abduction, the only stranger who is bad is the abductor. Everyone else is a possible rescuer and a friend.

One very sad but true fact is that a lot of people will not get involved in an emergency and help someone in need. How terrible it would be if your child were to free him or herself from an abductor and go to a stranger for help, only to be refused or not believed. Therefore, it is important to teach the child not only the right way to approach a stranger, but also, if possible, who the best strangers are to approach.

In a Public Place

First, go behind any counter where there is an employee (the parent should show the child how to get behind a counter when they're in a store together). Try to avoid empty counters. Tell the clerk "Help, I've been kidnapped!" Grab the clerk around the leg and do not let go. Keep repeating "Help, I've been kidnapped."

If going behind a counter is not possible, then grab hold of the first person you can and hold tightly while telling him or her loudly, "Help, I've been kidnapped." In a restaurant you can grab the waitress as she comes to the table. At a gas station, you can get into someone else's car.

Sometimes grabbing someone is not possible or does not work. Grown-ups don't always believe children. Remember what happened in the Jeffrey Dahlmer case when one of his young victims escaped and asked two police officers for help. The young boy was bleeding and terrified, yet the police did not believe him and returned him to his abductor who later dismembered the child.

When the child can't get help, he or she should run through the place pulling merchandise off the shelves letting it crash to the floor. Keep doing this until someone restrains you. Do this if an abductor tries to drag you out of a public place to kidnap you. Pulling merchandise off the shelf will alert the manager who could call the police or restrain the child.

Explain the following to your child. Vandalism is wrong under normal conditions. But when something wrong is happening to you such as being abducted, vandalism is acceptable and it may be your only chance to summon help. Vandalism alerts management, other people and the police. These people are a great source of help to save you from harm. They will be mad when they see you making a mess, but they will be glad when they find out you were making the mess because you needed their help.

On the Street

If the child can get free of the abductor "on the street," teach the child to run into and against the direction of pedestrians. The crowd acts as a natural obstacle for the abductor giving chase. Also, the child can move more easily and faster than most abductors in this environment. Teach the child to run into a store or any public place and use the attention-getting tactics mentioned in the previous section.

If there are not crowds, running the opposite direction of traffic can be effective, especially at night. The lights from the cars make it harder for the pursuer to see. Also, the cars moving past are a bit disorienting. In the daytime, running against traffic allows the faces of the abductor and child to be seen by the drivers.

Make sure you and your child understand that breaking free is only half the battle. Finding a safe place and summoning help is the other half. Keep in mind the harder and longer the abductor has to pursue the child, the angrier he will become. If the child is caught he most likely will not get a second chance to escape. Therefore, when fleeing and especially when summoning help, teach your child to do it *aggressively*. In this situation, shyness and politeness are your child's worst enemies.

Fire Alarms

Teach your child that it is okay to use a fire alarm to summon help during an abduction. Show him or her how to trip a fire alarm, where they are usually located on the street and in buildings. Teach your child to find a hiding place near the alarm and to stay there after pulling the alarm until the police or firefighters show up, then go to them.

Bus

While fleeing in public, getting on a bus is an excellent route of escape. Teach your child how to board a bus and summon help. Teach him or her how to recognize bus stops. If possible, he or she should find a hiding place near a bus stop, then wait there for the bus and run onto it when it stops.

Car Alarms

Car alarms are a great tool for drawing attention. Most car alarms can be set off by pulling on the door handle or bouncing against the car. While on the street, if the child can free him or herself from the abductor, he or she can pull on car door handles until an alarm goes off, then hide somewhere near the car and wait for help to arrive.

I.D. Bracelet

Have an identification bracelet made for your child. It can be worn on the wrist or around the ankle. The bracelet should be light weight, similar to medical alert bracelets. On the back of the bracelet have the following information engraved. Name, telephone number including area code, and "missing child, reward."

This bracelet can be left or dropped anywhere by the child such as in a restaurant, grocery store, or even thrown out a vehicle at someone. The bracelet technique is best used when the child and abductor get to a house where it appears they are going to stay for a night or so. In this case, drop the bracelet outside before going in. Or, if it appears that they are not going to stop, the child should drop the bracelet somewhere on the second day of the abduction, preferably in a populated area like a city street.

In any case, the bracelet drop should only be used after several hours into the abduction. If found and reported, this provides the police with a direction of flight. If someone finds the bracelet and calls you, make sure you get the following information:

• Exactly where it was found, city, state and address
• The name, phone number and address of the person who found the bracelet
• Time and date of the finding
• Offer the caller a one hundred dollar reward to be paid only after the police have received the bracelet

It would be a good idea to put a special mark somewhere on the bracelet so you can verify its authenticity.

Debbie

Debbie is nine years old. She was at a large department store clothes shopping with her mother and aunt when she was abducted.

Her aunt had been trying on a pair of pants. Her mother was standing about five feet away from her looking at a dress when a man grabbed Debbie. They disappeared into a crowd of shoppers.

It all happened so fast Debbie didn't have time to think. The man quickly pushed her into a corner where no one could see them. He showed Debbie a badge and told her he was a policeman protecting her from a kidnapper who was going to try to get her. He said he was taking her to a safe place in the store and another policemen was going to bring her mother to them.

Debbie didn't believe him. Her parents had told her about things like this happening to other children. She quickly pulled out of his grasp and ran into a crowd of people.

The abductor pursued her but could not move through the crowd as quickly as she could.

Debbie ran and soon found herself in the men's clothing department. She saw a rack with men's pants hanging on it. The rack was circular with pants hanging all around it. Debbie stepped into the center of the rack to hide.

The abductor searched for her for about ten minutes. He got scared thinking that she may have already found the police so he left the store.

After about twenty minutes, Debbie heard her name being called over the loud speaker, telling her to go to the nearest cashier and to tell them to call security. Debbie still did not leave her hiding place.

Eventually a store employee saw her and called security.

Debbie's mother and aunt were at the security office. They had been looking for her everywhere.

Debbie and her mother were reunited. The abductor was not found.

Chapter 5

How and When to Disable
a Molester or Abductor

A child trying to disable an adult is a risky bet with the odds favoring the adult. Disabling an adult can be done, but how and when are crucial.

If the child hurts the adult but fails to escape, the adult could be angry enough to retaliate by seriously injuring or killing the child. On the other hand, the abductor might just do that anyway.

The act of molestation may be a death sentence to the child whether or not the child fights back. For example, the molester could be infected by the HIV virus which causes AIDS. In Roseberg, Oregon, a man infected with AIDS took out his frustration and sought revenge on society by molesting the neighborhood children. He had been well liked by the parents in the neighborhood and was a preacher at the local church.

The children never fought back against his daily molestations which may have become deadly.

It should also be noted that many molesters murder their victims because they are either afraid the children will tell on them or they feel such a sense of guilt for what they have done that in their twisted mind, they blame the child and kill him or her as an act of atonement.

Before teaching your child to disable an abductor or molester, you've got to weigh the odds and consider the risks. It's hard to teach a child about justifiable violence when their child-like tendencies are and should be toward innocence, trust, and seeing the world through youthful optimism.

Teaching a child about justifiable violence is difficult because the child has a hard time separating justifiable from unjustifiable violence. To teach this lesson, it takes great diligence and persistence on the part of the parent. We don't want little Becky kicking Uncle Ned in the testicles just because he didn't tune the television to her favorite station.

However, if you as a parent feel that justifiable violence is morally right and may be effective in saving your child's life, then I offer the following suggestions.

When?

Choosing the right time to use violence against the molester or abductor is most important. The child must first have a guaranteed plan of escape before using violence against the molester -- a way out of the car or building and a place to go! The plan should include getting as far away as possible while the molester is recovering from injury. If possible the child should try to take the car keys with him or her and throw them somewhere along the way where they won't be found.

Escaping from a house is different when the molester is disabled than trying to sneak out without getting caught. Teach the child how to break out windows using objects and how to safely climb out. Teach them if there's time, dial 911 and leave the phone off the hook. Don't wait for an answer, just drop the receiver and go!

Escape must be swift. Stay out of the molester's reach. Again, no matter where the child is -- in a house or a vehicle -- escape must be guaranteed before using violence.

How to Disable a Molester

The techniques listed here are without a doubt violent. But so is rape. The point is to disable the molester in such a way as to allow the child to escape; not to hold the molester at bay. I would advise parents to enroll their child in a self-defense course.

Keep in mind that during the molestation the molester may be naked and preoccupied with the act itself which adds to his or her vulnerability. Both of these factors would work in favor of the child. Be sure to instruct your child that if he or she is naked when their chance for escape comes, don't get dressed first. Just go!

Sharp punch or kick to the testicles

If the molester has exposed his testicles to the child, teach the child to punch or kick the testicles as hard as possible. If possible, do it more than once. If the molester is a female, then the breast should be the target of the strike. The child can also bite the testicles or breast if hitting is not possible, but again, drawing blood has it's own inherent risks.

Poking or gouging the eyes

Show the child how to grab the hair on either side of the head and drive his or her thumbs into the molester's eyes as hard as possible.

Nose

If possible, the child can use his head to forcefully smash the molester in the nose. A blow to the nose could be followed by a punch to the testicles or gouging the eyes.

Tongue

If the molester puts his tongue into the child's mouth, instruct the child to bite it. Bite down as hard as possible. Unfortunately, if the molester has AIDS, this tactic would possibly cause serious problems to the child.

Ear

During the process of attack, if the child has access to biting the molester's ear, teach the child to get a big bite on the ear -- biting hard and not letting go. The child should shake his or her head violently back and forth like a dog does. This can possibly pull the ear out of the head (again, be advised of blood and AIDS).

If the molester is wearing earrings, pull them hard to tear the earlobes.

Sam

Sam is seven years old. His best friend Tony is eight. One day Sam and Tony were out in front of Tony's house riding their bikes when they decided to race around the block -- each one going a different way to see which one would get back to the house first. Tony got back to the house first, so he sat on his bike waiting for Sam. Sam never showed up. He's been missing now for three weeks. Sam was abducted by a man that likes to molest little boys. The man is holding Sam at a house which is only a few miles away from where Sam lives.

During the daytime, Sam is locked in a basement that has no windows. At night when the man gets home from work, he takes Sam upstairs and makes him stay in a bedroom. Every night the man goes into Sam's bedroom and makes him take off all his clothes. The man takes his clothes off too. The man touches Sam's private parts. He puts his penis in Sam's mouth and in his rectum. He makes Sam do the same thing to him.

Sam knows what the man is doing is wrong. When the man first started molesting Sam, he would cry and tell him to stop, but the man would beat him with a belt until he shut up. Now Sam closes his eyes and tries to think of ways to get away.

One day while Sam was sitting in the basement waiting for the man to get home, he remembered how once his friend Tony accidentally hit him in the testicles. He remembered how bad it hurt and all he could do was lay on the ground until his mother came to help him into the house. His mother scolded him and Tony about hitting people in that area and how dangerous it was. Sam's mother told him that the only time it was all right to hit someone there was if someone was trying to hurt him and he had to get away.

Sam thought to himself, "If I hit the man there when he has his clothes off, maybe I can get away while he's lying on the ground."

Later that night after the man came home and Sam was naked waiting for him in the bedroom, he decided that he was going to hit him in his testicles as hard as he could and then run away from the house.

The man came into the bedroom and took off his clothes. While he was standing in front of Sam naked, Sam made a fist and slugged the man in the testicles as hard as he could. The man grabbed his stomach and fell to the ground coughing and gagging. There was a deadbolt lock on the bedroom door which the man always locked and set the key on the dresser. Sam grabbed the key off the dresser carefully keeping watch on the man while unlocking the door. When Sam got out of the room, he locked the deadbolt from the other side and kept the key in his hand as he ran from the house.

Sam was naked but he didn't care, he just wanted to get away. About three houses down the street he saw a house with the lights on so Sam ran up to the front door and pounded on it screaming, "Help me, help me!"

A lady came to the door. When she saw Sam standing there naked she screamed. Sam ran past the lady into the house, right into the kitchen, and hid under the kitchen table.

Sam told the people what had happened to him and they called the police. When the police arrived, they went over to the molester's house. He was sitting on the floor in pain. They arrested him.

Sam was returned to his parents. He and his parents go to see a counselor every week and she helps Sam understand why the molester did the things he did to him. The counselor says Sam is going to make it, but it will take a long time.

Mary

Mary is nine years old. She has been missing for three months. She was abducted by a man who works with her father. The man took her from a Christmas party that her father's company had for the children. Mary knew the man because he sometimes played golf with her father.

The man keeps Mary at his house and has sex with her every night. The man tells Mary that if she has sex with him and does everything he tells her, then he will let her go home soon. Mary knows that the man is not going to let her go because her parents told her and her brothers about people like this. She knows that she's going to have to try and find a way out.

Whenever the man is gone, he gags Mary, puts handcuffs on her, and locks her in a closet. Sometimes he leaves the handcuffs on while he's having sex with her. Mary hasn't tried to escape yet because she's been too afraid. Mary thinks of lots of ways she could hurt the man but has been too afraid to try them. One day while she was locked in the closet she could hear the man talking on the telephone. She heard him say that it was time to get rid of the kid and find another one. Mary knew that he was planning to kill her. Although she was very scared, she knew it was time to try getting away.

Later that night when the man took her out of the closet to have sex with her, she could tell there was something different about the way he was acting. He was nervous and in a hurry. Mary also saw a knife on the night stand.

The man started to kiss her and as usual he put his tongue in her mouth. Something inside Mary snapped. While his tongue was in her mouth, she bit down as hard as she could. The man started to scream and tried to pull away. Mary bit down harder, reached up and grabbed his hair, and dug her thumbs into his eyes.

The man hit Mary in the side of her head causing her to let go and fall back onto the bed. The man fell to his knees holding his hands over this eyes and screaming. He was bleeding from his eyes and mouth. Mary jumped up from the bed and grabbed a lamp from the night stand and hit the man over the head, knocking him out.

Mary ran from the bedroom and called 911 from the living room. She was so scared she couldn't speak; she just cried and screamed "help me." The operator was able to trace the call to the man's address. When the police arrived, they found the man still unconscious in the bedroom.

Mary was taken to the hospital to be examined by the doctor. The police called Mary's parents. Later that night they were all together again.

Mary will not be the same person she was before the abduction, but she's alive and back with her family.

Chapter 6

Hiding Places

It's simple. If the child can free him or herself from the abductor then the smartest thing to do would be to run and tell someone what's happening. That person could call the police and stay with the child until the police arrive.

If the child is waiting with someone for the police and the abductor sees them, he wouldn't dare try recapturing the victim, right? Fat chance! On television the abductor gives up, but television and the real world are two different things.

Keep in mind, you're not dealing with a normal human adult. Child abductors are demented, twisted, monsters in every sense of the word. What normal human being could take pleasure in sexually abusing and mutilating a defenseless, innocent, and beautiful little child, taking pleasure in every painful scream? What normal human being would take a hatchet, a knife or a hammer to a child and enjoy every single blow or cut?

When I was a police officer, the hardest lesson I learned was the difference between the mind-set of the law-abiding citizen and the criminal. The criminal plays by a set of rules that law-abiding people don't even know exist.

Criminals take things to derive benefits from them. If it's cash they spend it, if it's goods they sell it, if it's a child they abuse and destroy it, and they waste no time accomplishing this morbid goal.

Criminal behavior is bizarre. Logic is not part of the equation. Let me repeat, criminals play by rules that most people don't even know exist.

Keep in mind that if a child is able to get away from an abductor, the abductor is most likely going to look for that child with the same intensity that you or I would as the parent. If you've ever lost a child, then you know how quickly panic sets in. Most people will begin to search for the child the instant they first realize he or she is missing.

If the child can get away from the abductor, having a good place to hide is extremely important. Upon freeing himself from the abductor, the faster the child finds a place to hide the better. As the abductor looks for the child, he will most likely move further and further away from where the child is hiding.

At this point the child is in control because he or she knows where they're hiding and the abductor does not. Some of the hiding places listed here can be used for immediate cover, which the child can then abandon for a better one if the abductor wanders away in his or her search. It is important however that the child find a good hiding place and stay there until it is safe to summon help.

If a child escapes from an abductor and is recaptured, he or she will probably never get another chance at freedom and may never be seen alive again.

Child abductors are not afraid of the police. If they were, they would not have taken the child in the first place. It's been known for abductors to enlist the help of store security or even the police in their effort to regain the child.

At least at this point the child is free and now in control. What's crucial is that he or she remain in control by a combination of making the right decisions and luck. The abductor will be searching and be in the general area. If the child has an opportunity to summon help then he or she should, but it must be done aggressively and convincingly as mentioned earlier in this book. If the child does not feel comfortable with summoning help, then he or she should stay hidden until he or she does feel comfortable. The longer the child is out of the abductor's grasp, the better the child's chances of rescue. Survival depends on instinct and instinct is developed by practice.

Potential Hiding Places

On the Street

• A garbage can or dumpster. Pull the garbage over him or herself while inside.

• Another vehicle. Lock the doors and lie down on the floor.

• In bushes.

• Under a bench.

• Under a vehicle. Avoid being in the path of the wheels should the car move.

• In a ditch.

• In a dark alley or dark doorway.

• In the back of a truck.

• In a crowd of people.

• In a stack of tires at a gas station or auto repair shop.

In a Public Place

- In the bathroom of the opposite sex of the abductor.
- Inside display counters (most counters have storage cabinets at the bottom).
- Inside or behind large appliances (exercise caution -- although some newer refrigerators and freezers can be safely opened from the inside, most cannot).
- Behind sales counters.
- Dressing rooms of the opposite sex of the abductor.
- Under a table.
- Inside racks of hanging clothes.
- In the stockroom behind boxes (show your child how to locate the stockrooms in every kind of store).
- In a restaurant kitchen.
- Behind floor-length curtains.

In the Country

- Under piles of leaves or inside overgrowth such as blackberry bushes or tall weeds.
- In a drain pipe under the roadway.
- Under a house or other structure.
- Up in a bushy tree.
- In a doghouse (but beware of dog).

- Go through a doggy door into a house (again, beware of dog).
- In a barn, behind or under hay.
- Under a bridge.
- If possible, somewhere close to mail boxes by the roadside in case someone comes along to pick up their mail and can help.
- In a hot water heater closet on the outside of a house.

In a House

- Under the sink.
- Inside the fireplace if it's summer.
- In a stack of laundry.
- Inside the closet and, if possible, on the upper shelf, behind boxes, or behind clothes.
- Behind a washer or dryer (but not inside).
- Inside cupboards or a rolltop desk.
- Inside a folded up roll-away bed.
- Inside a piano.
- Inside any large enough box.
- Laying flat under couch cushions.

These hiding places represent only a fraction of possible options for your child. After deciding which hiding places are right for your child, practice identifying and using them so your child feels confident should the need arise.

If your child were to need a hiding place, he or she should know to stay out of the open as much as possible. Don't stand in the center of an open area. Try to stay close to the walls of buildings. Find the best hiding place possible and stay there until someone comes who can help. Teach your child that it is okay to go to the bathroom in his or her pants while hiding.

A child could possibly stay hiding for a number of hours or days waiting for help. Teach your child how to find food and water while on his own, such as the from the following sources.

Where to Find Food and Water

• Animal food and water (dogs' and cats'). Be careful about taking food from animals; they could attack.

• Fruit and nut trees.

• Blackberries (warning:some berries can be poisonous).

• Water from hoses (teach them how to drink from a hose).

• Garbage cans. Teach them to smell first to tell whether the food is rotten.

Keeping Warm and Dry

If your child is exposed to the elements, he or she should know how to keep warm and dry. Tell them the following.

• Whenever possible, get under and/or behind a shelter such as a porch or a wall, bushy tree, car or fence; anything that will offer even the slightest bit of protection.

• Bundle up in a ball or fetal position to preserve body heat.

• Use cardboard, leaves, tree branches, or newspaper as covering and insulation from the cold and wet.

• Keep hands in pockets or pull arms inside the shirt for warmth.

• Jog in place to generate heat.

The bottom line is survival. Survival is not always attractive, but it beats the alternative. Teach your child how to employ extraordinary behavior in extraordinary circumstances.

Tim

Tim is nine years old. He's been missing now for four weeks. Tim was able to escape from the house where he was being held. He didn't know where he was, he didn't even know what state he was in or what day it was. All he knew was that he was somewhere out in the country and that the sun was starting to set.

Tim ran to a field across the road from the house. The field was overgrown with weeds and grass. He ran into the tall grass so he couldn't be seen. As Tim moved further and further away from the house, he stayed in the tall grass and kept down low so he could stay hidden. He kept the road in sight so he wouldn't get lost.

Soon it was dark and very cold. The man who abducted Tim was searching for him, but Tim was being careful to stay off the roadway. Tim didn't have a coat and was wearing a short-sleeved shirt. He came upon a large oak tree and rested up against it to try and shelter himself from the cold wind. There was a lot of brush and leaves all around the tree, so Tim piled them around himself to make a covering to keep himself warm. He was very tired and soon fell asleep.

When Tim awoke in the morning, he continued to move; staying in the tall grass for cover and keeping the road in sight. After a couple hours he saw a row of mail boxes at the edge of the road. He hid in the grass about ten feet from the boxes. He thought maybe someone would come by who could help him.

Several cars came by but Tim was afraid to flag them down for help because one of them could be the abductor. As he sat there, it dawned on him that sooner or later the mail carrier would have to deliver the mail. A few hours later, the postal delivery truck pulled up to the mail boxes. Tim quickly ran to the truck and climbed inside the open door. The mail carrier was outside the truck stuffing boxes. When she returned to the truck she saw Tim on the floorboard. She was startled but asked what he was doing. Tim told her. She drove him straight to the sheriff's office.

The sheriff sent an officer to the house where Tim had been imprisoned. The abductor was there. He was brought to the sheriff's office for questioning. Tim identified him as his abductor. He was arrested on the spot and Tim ended up being returned safely to his parents.

Practice Makes Perfect

When I was growing up in the '60s, we practiced something in school called a "disaster drill." It was designed to teach the students how to react in case of a nuclear attack. We were instructed to push our desks against the wall with the windows, sit under our desks, pull our knees up to our chest and tuck our head into our knees. Year after year we practiced this drill until it was an automatic reaction when the alarm sounded. We did similar practices with fire drills. Even though I never experienced a nuclear attack or fire during my school days, I was prepared for the emergency.

The odds of a school kid being caught in a fire are no greater than the odds of being abducted. How many times has your child practiced an abduction drill? In our society we tend to shy away from unpleasant topics -- out of sight, out of mind does not make the abductor go away, it simply increases his or her chance of success.

Set aside some time with your child to talk about and practice the techniques in this book and from other sources. Be careful not to overload the child with information. Keep it simple. Practice each technique until it becomes an instinctive reaction for your child. Explain the reason for each technique.

The techniques listed for disabling a molester should be demonstrated cautiously so no one gets hurt during practice. Through practice, the child learns that he can be successful during a real situation.

Practice hiding, escaping, and other techniques at stores and restaurants, at neighbors' houses and on the street. Sit down with your child and make up a scenario of abduction, then go to a store, a restaurant or anywhere else and practice the maneuver until the child gets it right. Don't be embarrassed or timid. You can be sure the abductor won't be.

Chapter 7

Avoiding Abduction

- Read this book and discuss it with your child at an early age.
- The child should always be aware of his or her environment. Watch for anything unusual or different and stay away from the situation.
- Never tell a phone caller no one else is home. Instead, should the caller persist in knowing, tell the caller "Mom or Dad is unable to come to the phone right now, may I take a message?"
- Have your child photographed at least once a year; more often if under five years old.
- Tell your child that if he or she is home alone, do not open the door for anyone except people you have predetermined are okay to open the door for. A young child should never be left alone at home.

- Never let your young child go into a public restroom by him or herself.
- Pay attention to threats by an ex-spouse of stealing the child.
- Older children should come home at dark.
- Teach your child not to ride home from school with anyone, even if they say you told them to pick up the child.
- Do not walk over to a car whose occupants are asking for directions. Most adults do not ask children how to get places.
- Communicate with your child openly so he or she will feel comfortable telling you about problems and trouble.
- Keep fingerprints, footprints, and birth certificates of your child, as well as other means of identification.
- Get a passport for your child. That makes it difficult for someone else to get one for him or her. Contact the post office for information.
- Have your child be cautious if playing in deserted places.
- Have the child's school establish a School Call Back Program. This program requires the school to call the parent when the child is absent and the parent has not phoned the school within an hour stating the child will be absent. Otherwise the ab-

ductor could have all day before the child is known to be missing.

• Walk the neighborhood with your child. Pick the safest routes to school and friend's houses. Avoid alleys and places someone could be hiding. Discuss safe places to go in an emergency, such as certain neighbors or an open store.

• Teach your child if someone is trying to grab him or her, to scream, "Stay away from me" or "This person is trying to hurt me," and run to the nearest populated place.

• Teach your child how to recognize and trust their gut instincts. Identify the sick or fluttery feeling you get in your stomach whenever you know that some-thing is wrong or out of place. Abductors and molesters are masters at challenging and defeating this instinct.

• Abductors sometimes single one child out of an entire group and then set about to separate that child from the group. Instruct your child that if he or she is with a group to pay attention and not allow anyone to separate him or her from the rest.

• Never underestimate the cunning or forwardness of an abductor. Sometimes the greater the challenge, the more they are motivated. Abductors are not shy. They have been known to steal a child within plain sight of the parent, guardian or their friends.

• Establish a code word. This is a secret word known only to you, your child, and anyone you authorize to pick up your child. If someone tries to pick your child up from school or somewhere else and does not know and say the code word, then your child knows not to go with that person.

• Teach your child not to be fooled by old people. Sometimes old people are abductors. Also, don't be fooled by another child; some abductors use children to lure other children.

• Instruct your child that if an adult or any stranger is hanging around some place where the child is, to go to a safer place.

• Teach your child never to let another adult take pictures of him or her if you're not there.

• Teach your child to be punctual. Make sure he or she has a watch and knows how to tell time. Constantly reinforce the fact that being on time is extremely important. This serves two purposes. One, if children know they have to pay attention to time, they are more likely to be aware of where they are and less likely to stray, in order not to be late. Secondly, if your child establishes a reputation for being on time, then if he or she is late coming home or getting somewhere, then the red flags will go up quickly. If a child is in trouble, time means everything.

As the parent or guardian, you should never be timid or made to feel embarrassed about calling the police if you think your child is too late or in trouble. Better safe than sorry. Embarrassment will fade with time. Regret over having done nothing will be much harder to live with if the worst has happened.

If your child does not want to be around certain adults, even if you don't understand why they feel that way, pay close attention. Your child may be trying to tell you something about that person the only way he or she knows how. Just because your child might not want to be around a certain person doesn't mean that person has done anything wrong. On the other hand, it may mean exactly that.

Latch Key Kids

Latch Key is the term used to describe children that are usually home alone for a period of time after school until their parents or parent gets home from work. Although this may not be a desireable situation, for many families it may be their only choice. In this type of situation, make sure that your child checks in with you or another responsible adult at a specific time every day. Make sure that the child checks in at the same time each day, so that a definite pattern is established. If the child does not check in with the adult, then there should be no time wasted in calling the authorities.

Chapter 8

What to Do if a Child is Missing

If you have reason to believe your child may be missing, then a definite plan of action must be taken immediately. Don't waste any time.

If you think your child may be at a friend's house, then call that number. If your child is not there, then follow this emergency missing child action plan.

FIRST: Call 911 and tell the person who answers the phone that you are reporting a possible missing child. Tell him or her that this is a high priority police emergency. He or she will start asking you some questions. Try to remain calm and answer the questions as completely as possible. The operator will be relaying this information to the officers on the street even while you're talking, so action will already be under way.

SECOND: When you hang up with the police, immediately call the nearest missing children organization in your area. This is not a time to be searching for phone numbers. You should already have this number written down in a safe place. The people who staff these organizations will know exactly what to do and will jump into action immediately.

THIRD: Contact the Center for Missing and Exploited Children. This is a clearing house for missing children and they have the ability to get the word out about your child coast to coast. Their number is 1-800-843-5678. This number should also be written down and kept in a safe place. The national center can also put you in touch with a local missing children organization in your area.

FOURTH: Contact your local sheriff's department search and rescue division. Call them yourself and request that they get involved in the search for your child.

FIFTH: Contact the F.B.I. Missing Children Task Force. Their phone number should be listed in the front of your phone book.

After all these agencies have been notified, then contact the media -- radio, television and newspaper.

All of these numbers should be written on a card and kept near the phone and on your person, as would any emergency number.

Dignity Memorial® is a network of funeral, cremation and cemetery service providers throughout the United States and Canada. Additional Escape School® books and videos may be ordered from your local Dignity Memorial provider. To locate your local Dignity Memorial funeral service provider, visit www.DignityMemorial.com.

To view available Escape School materials visit www.escapeschool.com. To schedule a presentation in your area, contact your local Escape School instructor. Escape School instructors can be located through www.escapeschool.com/other/instruct.